SYMPHONIES DE BEETHOVEN

Partition de Piano

dédiées au Baron H. de Bülow

par

F. LISZT.

Vol. II.

Arrangement propriété des éditeurs.

Leipzig, Breitkopf & Härtel.

Pr. 9 Mark netto.

12172. II.

Beethoven Symphonies Nos. 6–9

Transcribed for Solo Piano by
FRANZ LISZT

Introduction by
Alan Walker

DOVER PUBLICATIONS, INC.
Mineola, New York

Bibliographical Note

This Dover edition, first published in 2001, is an unabridged republication of Volume II of *Symphonies de Beethoven / Partition de Piano / dediée au Baron H. de Bülow par F. Liszt*, originally published by Breitkopf & Härtel, Leipzig [1865]. The frontispiece, annotated contents list, glossary and main headings are newly added.

Dr. Alan Walker graciously provided the following materials, drawn or adapted from portions of his three-volume work *Franz Liszt*, originally published by Alfred A. Knopf, New York, in 1983, 1989 and 1996: an introduction to the Dover edition; and a facsimile of Liszt's handwritten French preface to his Beethoven transcriptions, together with its English translation.

International Standard Book Number: 0-486-41884-7

Manufactured in the United States of America
Dover Publications, Inc., 31 East 2nd Street, Mineola, N.Y. 11501

CONTENTS

Liszt's piano transcriptions of Beethoven's nine symphonies were originally published by Breitkopf & Härtel, Leipzig, in 1865. The complete edition was dedicated to conductor and virtuoso pianist Hans von Bülow, Liszt's favorite student, later his son-in-law. Humphrey Searle catalogued the complete set of transcriptions as S464; Peter Raabe, as R376.

LISZT AND THE BEETHOVEN SYMPHONIES

Between June 1863 and April 1865, while in devotional studies in his small cell at the Oratory of the Madonna del Rosario, outside Rome, Liszt brought to completion his remarkable series of piano transcriptions of the Beethoven symphonies. Perhaps the most piquant part of the business was that much of the creative work was done on an antiquated *pianino* (with a missing D!), and the first ears to hear the strains of these arrangements were those of the Domenican brothers. On April 25, Liszt received the tonsure at the Vatican—a major turning-point in his life—and entered Holy Orders. He even lived in the Vatican for a time, and that is where he checked the proofs of these transcriptions.

The task of transcription had occupied Liszt, off and on, for nearly thirty years. In 1836—in his heyday as a young virtuoso, and single-mindedly devoted to the memory of Beethoven—Liszt had begun work on the Fifth Symphony, possibly with little thought that he might one day tackle the entire set. But by 1839 he had completed the Fifth, Sixth and Seventh Symphonies, as well as the Funeral March from the "Eroica," premiering his transcription of the "Pastorale" in Vienna with such success that it would become something of a recital warhorse with him.

The impulse to complete the entire set came from the publishers Breitkopf & Härtel. Aware of what Liszt had already accomplished, they urged him to tackle the other works. Liszt agreed, on condition that he be allowed to revise his earlier efforts and issue all nine symphonies together. To help him get started, Breitkopf sent Liszt the orchestral scores in their own "critically revised" editions.

Nobody understood the art of transcription better than Liszt, yet even he regarded these symphonies as a difficult prospect for one pair of hands. In his preface to the collection [*see p. xi*] he declared his aims:

> . . . I shall think my time well spent if I have succeeded in transfer-
> ring to the piano not only the grand outlines of Beethoven's com-
> positions but also those multitude of details and finer points that
> make such a significant contribution to the perfection of the whole.

What gripped his imagination was the challenge these symphonies represented in defying ten fingers to reproduce them *without harming Beethoven's thought*. The results were spectacular, a model of their kind: the transcriptions remain unsurpassed in the amount of fine orchestral detail incorporated into their texture, and their solutions—often of seemingly impossible technical problems—are carried out in the most pianistic way. One need only compare Liszt's solutions to those that preceded him: Kalkbrenner's (in 1840), Hummel's (before 1837) and, above all, Czerny's (1827–9). As a function of his art, Liszt understood that a liberty judiciously taken could bring the "truth" of a passage more directly to the listener: "In matters of translation," he once remarked, "there are some exactitudes that are the equivalent of infidelities."

Nowhere is this thought more evident than in Liszt's transcriptions of the last three symphonies. As we enter Beethoven's final creative period his orchestral writing becomes more intense, his instrumental textures more complex. When Liszt accepted Breitkopf's commission, he had warned the publisher that however brilliant the arrangements, they would always remain "a very poor and distant *approximation*" [his italics] because of the limitations of the piano. "How to instill into the futile hammers of the piano the breath and soul, the resonance and power, the fullness and inspiration, the color and accent" of such music?[1] At every touch and turn the transcriber is beset with the problem of how to render the transfers to the keyboard with precision. A simple example can stand for the others. The opening of the Finale of Symphony no. 8 (p. 115) beckons the would-be arranger into a veritable quicksand, in which he is likely to flounder without recourse to some creative re-thinking. Beethoven's rapidly reiterated notes on the first and second violins, a simple enough device on stringed instruments, cannot be reproduced on the piano. Liszt's solution is to write an oscillating figure of triplets which creates the illusion of a direct transfer. The faster you play it, in fact, the better it sounds. Liszt also cues in the various orchestral instruments in order to give the performer some idea of the *timbre* he is striving to conjure from the keyboard. His fingerings, too, provide some stimulating solutions to otherwise intractable technical problems.

It was in the Chorale Finale of the Ninth Symphony, however, that even Franz Liszt went down to defeat. He wrote to Breitkopf:

> After various endeavours one way and another, I became inevitably and distinctly convinced of the impossibility of making any pianoforte arrangement of the fourth movement *for two hands,* that could in any way be even approximately effective or satisfactory.[2]

He begged Breitkopf to consider his work of transcription finished with the conclusion of the third movement of the Ninth. Breitkopf refused to be brushed aside, however, and Liszt reluctantly returned to the task. In his letter of compliance, he characteristically fell back on a proverb to express the dilemma facing him: "So often goes the pitcher to water that at last it is filled." It never was quite filled, however. Liszt openly acknowledges his difficulty by printing the choral parts on separate staves above the transcribed orchestral score. While the music is at such times strictly unplayable, deployed as it is across four staves, it has the great advantage of keeping Beethoven's intentions with regards to the chorus absolutely clear.

There is a revealing postscript to Liszt's Beethoven symphony transcriptions. Two years after they were published, Breitkopf & Härtel invited Liszt to tackle the string quartets—ostensibly a far simpler task. In October 1866 he wrote to the firm, after having wrestled with the pieces for several months:

1. Franz Liszt's Briefe, vol. 2, p. 35
2. op. cit., p. 76.

> It is very mortifying to me to have to confess that I have most awkwardly come to a standstill with the transcription of the Beethoven Quartets. After several attempts the result was either absolutely *unplayable*—or *insipid* stuff. Nevertheless, I shall not give up my project, and shall make another attempt to solve this problem of pianoforte arrangement. If I succeed I will at once inform you of my "Eureka."[3]

He never did succeed. The reason, as his letter makes clear, was his unwillingness to publish anything unplayable. As for the playable, that was merely pointless to him where the result was simply to obscure Beethoven's intentions. Time and again, these are the principles on which Liszt refuses to yield. They raise his transcriptions above the humdrum level of the mere "piano reduction" to that of great art.

In the decades that have elapsed since their publication, these Beethoven transcriptions have developed a wide following. Sir Donald Francis Tovey said of them that they "prove conclusively . . . that Liszt was by far the most wonderful interpreter of orchestral scores on the pianoforte the world is ever likely to see."[4] In times past, they used to be likened to gramophone records of the nineteenth century—there to be played in the absence of a symphony orchestra. But Edison has meanwhile invented the gramophone, and these transcriptions have not been displaced. In fact, they have taken on new life and have themselves been recorded.

When the nine symphony transcriptions were finally published, they appeared with a dedication to Liszt's greatest pupil, Hans von Bülow. It was a fitting gesture. Bülow was even then widely regarded as the greatest Beethoven interpreter after Liszt, and he had often conducted these symphonies in public—as had Liszt himself in earlier times. And when, a few years later, Bülow published his famous edition of the Beethoven Sonatas, he dedicated them in turn to "My Master Franz Liszt, as the fruits of his teaching."

Alan Walker

Dr. Alan Walker is author of *Franz Liszt*, a work in three volumes: *The Virtuoso Years, 1811–1847; The Weimar Years, 1848–1861;* and *The Final Years, 1861–1886.* The volumes were published by Alfred Knopf, New York, in 1983, 1989 and 1996, respectively; and by Cornell University Press, New York, in 1987, 1993 and 1997. Dr. Walker is also the editor of *Schumann: The Man and the Musician* (Barrie & Jenkins Ltd., London, 1972) and of *The Chopin Companion* (W. W. Norton, New York, 1973). He is on the faculty of The School of the Arts, McMaster University, Hamilton, Ontario, Canada.

---

3. op. cit., pp. 94–95.
4. Essays in Musical Analysis, vol. 1, p. 193.

A facsimile page of Liszt's preface
to his piano transcriptions of the Beethoven symphonies

(Courtesy of Alan Walker)

PREFACE

The name of Beethoven is sacred in art. His symphonies are nowadays universally recognized to be masterpieces. No one who seriously desires to extend his knowledge, or create something new himself, can ever devote sufficient thought to them, or ever study them enough. That is why every way of making them widely known and popular has some merit; not that the rather numerous arrangements published so far are without a certain merit, though for the most part deeper study readily reduces their value. The poorest lithograph, the faultiest translation, always gives an idea, however vague, of the genius of a Michelangelo and of a Shakespeare; and even the most imperfect piano arrangement will now and then reveal traces, a little obliterated perhaps, of a master's inspiration. But the advances the piano has gained of late, in both the technique of performance and in mechanical improvement, make it possible to produce more and better arrangements than ever before. As a result of the vast development of its harmonic power, the piano is trying more and more to take possession of all orchestral compositions. Within the compass of its seven octaves it is capable, with but a few exceptions, of reproducing all the features, all the combinations, and all the configurations of the deepest musical creations. And it leaves to the orchestra no other advantages than those of contrasting tone colors and mass effects—immense advantages, to be sure.

Such has been my aim in the work I lay before the public today. I confess that I should have to regard it as a rather useless employment of my time if I had produced just another version of the Symphonies in a manner up to now routine. But I shall think my time well spent if I have succeeded in transferring to the piano not only the grand outlines of Beethoven's compositions but also those multitude of details and finer points that make such a significant contribution to the perfection of the whole. I will be satisfied if I stand on the level of the intelligent engraver, or the conscientious translator, who grasps the spirit of a work and thus contributes to our insight into the great masters and to our sense of the beautiful.

Franz Liszt
Rome, 1865
Translated from the original French by Alan Walker

GLOSSARY
Orchestral instrument names and other terms in the piano score

Alto(s) = violas

Basses = contrabasses (string bases) [also see *C.B.*]
Basson(s) = bassoon(s)

Celli(s) [also see *Violonc.*]
C. B. [*Contrebasses*] = contrabasses (string basses)
Clar(inette) = clarinet
Cors = French horns

et = end

Flute(s), Fl.

Hauth(ois) = oboe

Instr(uments) à cordes, I. à c. = stringed instruments
Instr(uments) à vent, I. à v. = wind instruments

Péd(ale) à chaque mesure = separate pedal for each measure
pizz(icato) = plucked
pour le Piano à 7 octaves = for a 7-octave piano [*see p. 190*]

seul(s) = alone

Timb(ales) = timpani (kettle drums)
 (appears once as *Timballes*)
Tous l'orchestre, Tutti = full orchestra
Trombones
Tromp(ettes) = trumpets

Viola [also see *Alto*]
Viol., Violons = violins
 (appears once as the German *Violinen*)
Violonc(elles) = cellos

FOOTNOTES IN THE SCORE

p. 78, first system
The horn motif in the bass should be *piano* but accented.

p. 78, last system
The entire movement (including the contrasting D-major section) to be repeated.

p. 115, footnote
The articulation of the orchestra's leading motif is not [example] but [example] or [example].
Therefore, the pianist should observe the last version in all occurences of the motif.

p. 164, 4th system
The accompanying parts should be even *pp* and *staccato*; the leading motif, *legato*.

p. 166, last system
(The horn part somewhat emphasized.)

p. 167, 3rd system
The accompanying parts in the left hand should always be even *pp* and *staccato*.

p. 187, above last six measures
"These six measures may be omitted by the soloist, but not by the chorus."
[Beethoven's original instructions in the full score]

Beethoven Symphonies
Nos. 6–9
Transcribed for Solo Piano

Symphony No. 6

in F Major, Op. 68 ("Pastorale") (1808)

Erwachen heiterer Empfindungen bei der Ankunft auf dem Lande.

Allegro ma non troppo. ($\dot{o}$ = 66.)

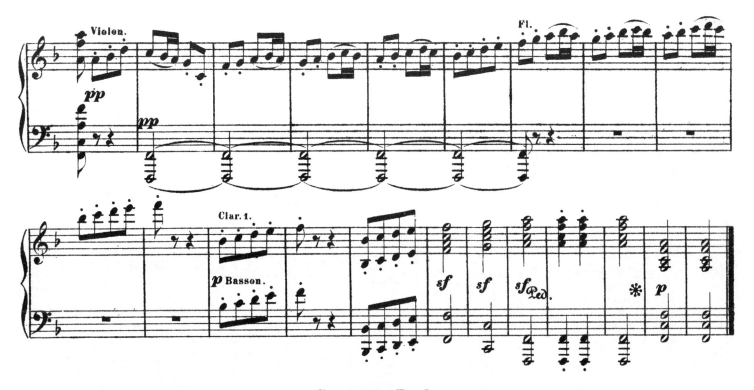

Scene am Bach.

Lustiges Zusammensein der Landleute.

Donner. Sturm.

Symphony No. 6 (IV) 31

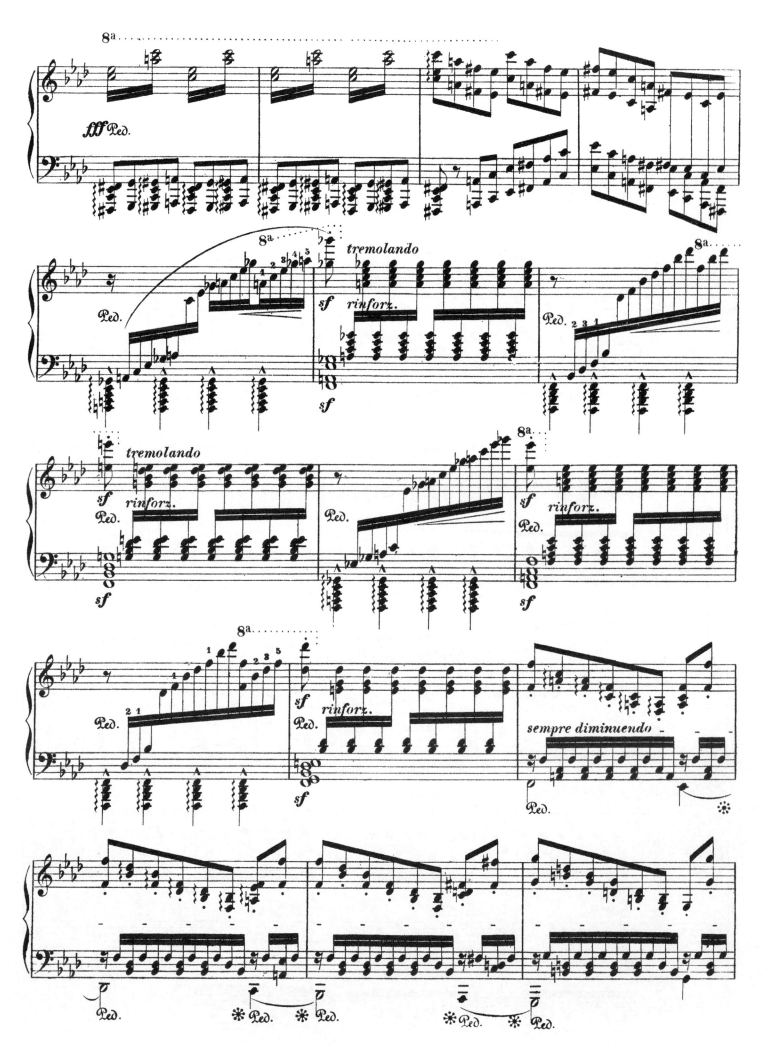

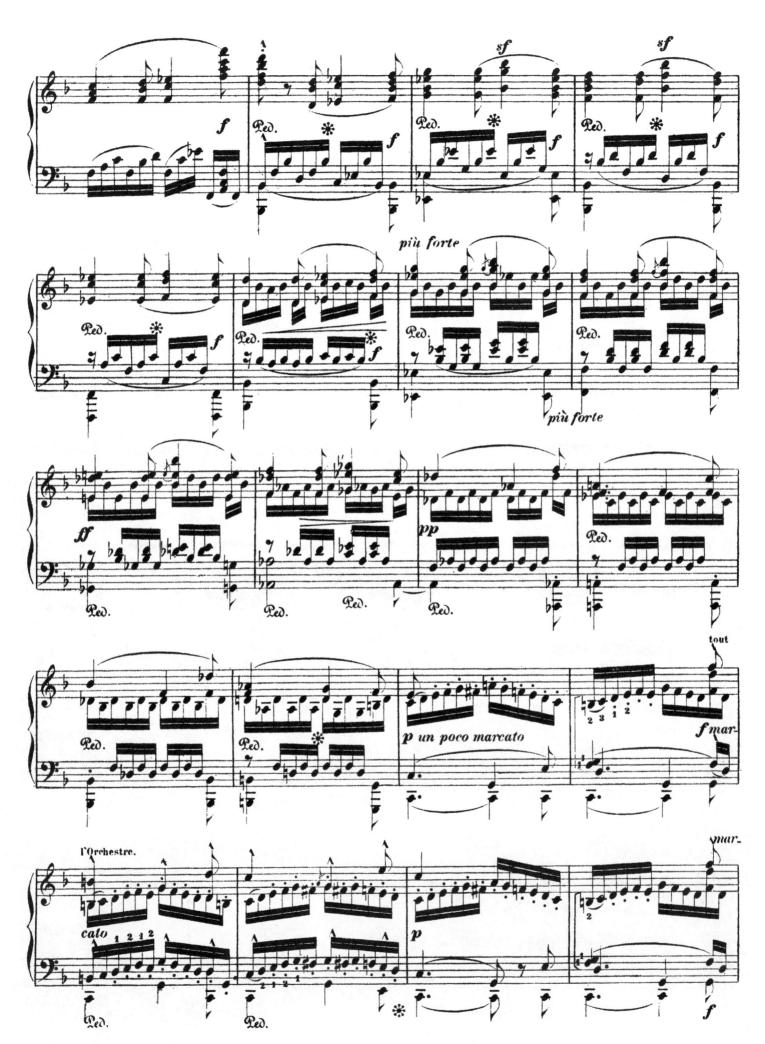

Orchestral score dedicated to
Count Moritz von Fries

Symphony No. 7

in A Major, Op. 92 (1811-12)

Ossia.

Ossia.

Symphony No. 8

in F Major, Op. 93 (1812)

104   Symphony No. 8 (I)

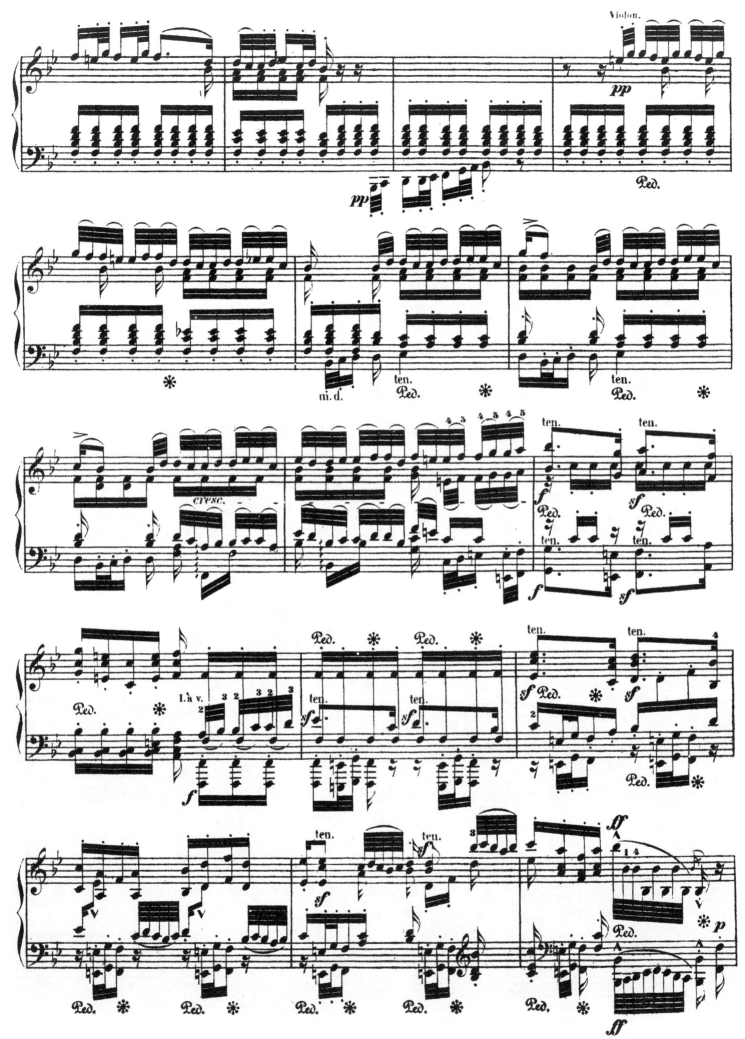

⁺⁾ Der Vortrag der Hauptfigur des Motivs im Orchester ist nicht ♪♪♪ sondern ♪♪♪ oder ♪♪♪ demnach hat der Clavier-spieler letztere Bezeichnung bei allen Motivstellen zu befolgen.

Symphony No. 9

in D Minor, Op. 125 ("Choral") (1822–24)

148   Symphony No. 9 (I)

Adagio molto e cantabile.

NB. Die begleitenden Stimmen gleichmässig *pp* und staccato; die Figurirung des Gesang's legato.

NB. Die begleitenden Stimmen der linken Hand immer gleichmässig *pp* und staccato.

NB. Diese 6 Takte können nicht vom Chor wohl aber vom Solo-Sänger ausgelassen werden.

196   Symphony No. 9 (IV)